MW01056420

The Complete Alkaline Diet Cookbook for Beginners:

Understand pH, Eat Well with Easy Alkaline Diet Cookbook and More Than 50 Delicious Recipes

10 Day Meal Plan.

Contents

Chapter 1.

What is the Alkaline Diet?

Every health specific dietary plan is created to produce somewhat similar results, yet each follows a different road to achieve such objectives. The Alkaline Diet has been brought out about by the experts to help our body work effectively and efficiently while curbing the threats of many diseases. This is because the human body requires an optimum pH level for all the enzymes to actually work. The neutrality of the internal environment can be maintained only with a good and balanced diet. Since most of the food products are more acidic in nature, we all suffer from ailments like gut acidity, indigestion, and other related diseases. The alkaline diet is the answer to all such problems as it gives you a right approach to maintain the internal pH level.

What is pH?

In simple words, pH indicates the level of acidity in a substance. The lower the pH values, the high the acidity is. The entire pH scale ranges from 1 to 14 in values. Substances with pH value smaller than 6 are termed as acidic. PH 7 indicates neutrality and any value higher then this is termed as alkaline. The greater the value, the more alkaline the substance is.

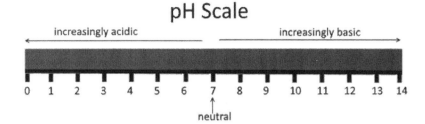

pH Scale

increasingly acidic   increasingly basic

0 1 2 3 4 5 6 7 8 9 10 11 12 13 14

neutral

The food we eat also varies in its pH value; some substances are rich in acids whereas others are more alkaline. There are no marked categories to distinguish a pure alkaline diet from a nonalkaline one, except to identify the items with low pH and avoid them. Items like lemons, oranges, meat, dairy and processed food, all are acidic in nature. Here are some pH value of the commonly used food items to give you a basic idea about pH and its relation to food.

Food	pH values
lemon juice	2.00–2.60
limes	2.00–2.80
blue plums	2.80–3.40
grapes	2.90–3.82
pomegranates	2.93–3.20
grapefruits	3.00–3.75
blueberries	3.12–3.33
pineapples	3.20–4.00
apples	3.30–4.00
peaches	3.30–4.05
oranges	3.69–4.34

tomatoes	4.30–4.90
sauerkraut	3.30–3.60
cabbage	5.20–6.80
beets	5.30–6.60
corn	5.90–7.50
mushrooms	6.00–6.70
broccoli	6.30-6.85
collard greens	6.50–7.50

How Food Affects Your Body

Food serves more than just a mere source of energy; it provides the necessary components to maintain a hospitable environment inside the body to allow each and every organ work in complete sync and harmony. Hence, the type of food is a preliminary factor in carrying out all bodily functions effectively. It strengthens our immune system, fights with diseases, strengthens muscles and aids constant growth. Acidic food is not only harmful to the stomach but also for other internal organs. Alkaline food in comparison is simpler to digest and keeps up the internal pH balance of the body.

Why the Alkaline Diet Helps

The science behind alkaline food is that it has higher pH levels and simpler ingredients. Once we intake food, it passes through a series of digestive processes, experiences changing pH environments, and finally breaks down into energy molecules. Most of the enzymes in our digestive system, except for stomach, requires alkaline and or neutral environment to work on food molecules. Unavailability of such food can cause indigestion, the death of many gut microbes and inhibit absorption of a number of nutrients. Alkaline diet neutralizes the gastric juices and helps in better digestion throughout the gut.

Proof that the alkaline diet is useful

The idea of the alkaline surfaced with the observation of some experts claiming certain food items as more acid-forming than the other. These food items release more calcium from the bones and end up causing osteoporosis in early ages. Further studies later revealed that it is not just a few items, rather a number of items having low pH, which are linked to diseases like bone weakness, cancer, heart strokes, gut ailments, diabetes, bloating, headaches, etc.

The alkaline diet came to much use as prevention of kidney stones and urinary infections. There are a number of scientific researches and studies which support such claims. Group of people who switched to alkaline food, experienced less acidity, high metabolic rates, strong bones and muscles over the time period of few months.

Microbiome and its role in alkalinity

As we all know, there is a number of microbes including some bacteria which resides inside our gut. These microbes aid the digestion process protects the inner lining of the intestine and helps in better absorption of food. The microbiome is a complete habitat which is created by these microbes inside our guts. They release enzymes which breakdowns food, otherwise not digested by the body and removes all the toxins. Such microbes can better thrive in the alkaline environment. Providing more alkaline food and liquid to the body mean strengthening these microbiomes and maintain their growth inside.

The ratio of macros and how that affects alkalinity

The ratio of macros indicates the amount of energy obtained from different macronutrients present in the food, i.e., protein, carbohydrates, and fats. A basic understanding of macros gives a complete view of the type of the food item we take and the type we should be taking instead to bring better changes within the body. How the ratios of these nutrients relate to the alkalinity of the body is the question which takes us to the chemistry of these macros. Take protein, for instance; these are the complexed organic molecules which contain amino acids. Break down of these long chains, produces aminos, urea, and uric acid. Thus, a diet rich in protein like meats and dairy is termed as acidic and hence forbidden on an alkaline diet. The lesser the proteins, the better the alkaline diet will be.

Carbohydrates, on the other hand, are more diverse in their forms and structure. A high dose of carbs, like that in sugars and beans, are acid forming in nature. However, other forms of it, present in some vegetables and fruits, are alkaline forming. Thus it is prescribed to go for a balanced approach while taking in carbohydrates.

Fats are composed of fatty acids and glycerides. Unsaturated fats like vegetable oils and ghee are more alkaline then animal fats.

Keeping in consideration the amount of alkalinity each macro hold, we can decide their daily intake. Lesser proteins, a moderate amount of carbs and selective fats, constitutes the possible approach for an alkaline diet.

Chapter 2: How to Follow the Alkaline Diet

Health Conditions Improved By Eating a More Alkaline Diet

Though we cannot chalk a complete map which could relate the direct link between the alkaline diet and the cure of various diseases, the effects of alkaline diet on people suffering from following ailments were revolutionary. Within a period of one year, a strict alkaline diet can help strive a person against the threats of these diseases:

Arthritis:

It's a bone-related disorder where the lack of calcium and other mineral causes the degeneration of bone cartilages and coverings. This results in pain and swelling in the joints and immobility of the bones. Alkaline diet stops the release of excessive calcium in the body as it neutralizes the effects of acid produced. Thus, helping to improve the bone structure and makes them stronger.

Diabetes:

The release of hormones and their critical balance is also controlled by the blood pH levels. Lesser Blood pH levels mean lesser production of Insulin in the blood, causing diabetes. Alkaline food is, therefore, a long-term solution to control the blood sugar and the blood pH level.

Cancer:

Acidic food destroys all the protective microbes inside our gut which otherwise ingest cancer-causing elements in the body. Alkaline food, therefore, protects those bacteria while indirectly protecting the entire body from cancer-causing agents.

Insomnia:

Most of the toxins produced inside the body are acidic radicals which damage the brain cells, neurotransmitters, and the whole sleep cycle of a person. Alkaline food neutralizes those toxins and the blood which cures insomnia to some extent.

Muscle Pain:

You must have heard of the accumulation of acid in the muscle cells, which leads to pain after a random workout or some routine activities. Alkaline diet also neutralizes the effects of lactic acid produced as a result of anaerobic respiration in the muscles, curing pain and muscle weakness.**Gout:**

Gout is a disease which is caused by the accumulation of uric acid in the body. Alkaline food can help reduce the level of uric acid and can prevent gout threats. It is safe to switch to the alkaline diet, especially when you want to avoid medications.

Bloating:

Acid forming food cause more acidity in the stomach and cause stomach bloating. Alkaline food prevents bloating.

Alkaline water?

Regular drinking water has the pH level of 7 which is considered neutral. Water having a higher pH level than 7 is termed as Alkaline Water. It has the pH value of 8 to 9. As acid forming food has become the greater part of our lives, alkaline water has been brought into use for its following beneficial effects and easier intake:

- Prevention of cancer
- Strengthens the immune system
- Weight loss
- Anti-aging effects
- Detoxification

Alkaline Diet Frequently Asked Questions

Q. Can Alkaline Foods Help with Acid Reflux?

It is a fact that there is a direct link between Acid reflux and alkaline food. Alkaline food items can cause neutralization of the HCL produced inside the stomach. If a person is suffering from constant acid reflux, a switch to the alkaline diet can prove to be miraculous in such case.

Q. Can Alkaline Foods Help You Lose Weight?

Alkaline foods are low on sugars, complexed fats, and proteins. This is the reason that it can cause weight loss and maintains it as desired. It also prohibits the use of processed and fermented food which are the main causes of obesity these days.

Q. Can You Cook Alkaline Foods?

Cooking alkaline food doesn't make them acidic. However, if you add side ingredients which are acid forming in nature, then this may turn the alkaline ingredients into acidic ones. Excessive cooking also leads to loss of nutrients and minerals. Cooking to such an extent should be avoided.

Q. Can an Alkaline Diet Help with Allergies?

Allergic reactions are most often caused by particles which proved to be toxic for the body. Whether it's pollen, dust, or another form of allergies, alkaline diet has proved to be helpful in curbing the effects of allergens on the body.

Q. Can an Alkaline Diet Help with Acne?

Unhealthy, greasy, and sugary food is among the few the causes of acne. Lower blood pH can also cause skin breakouts. In this regard, an alkaline diet can help in preventing or treating acne of various kinds.

Alkaline- and Acid-Forming Foods

Based on the by-products, each food item produces while digestion, they are divided into two main categories, The Acid Forming foods and The Alkaline Forming Food. Acid forming foods release molecules which are acidic in nature they likely produced substances like uric acid, amino acid, etc. Contrary to this, alkaline food produces by-products which have neutralizing effects:

Acid-Forming Foods

Down below is the complete list of Acid forming food items:
- All meat: beef, pork, lamb, fish and chicken
- Rice : white, brown, or basmati
- Cornmeal, rye
- Popcorn
- Pasta
- Cheese
- Wheat germ
- Colas
- Alcoholic drinks
- Coffee and other caffeinated drinks
- Sweetened yogurt
- Refined table salt
- Soy sauce

- Mustard
- Ketchup
- Mayonnaise
- White vinegar
- Nutmeg
- Tobacco

Alkalinizing Foods

Item producing more bicarbonates are termed as Alkalinizing and forms the following list:

- Beans such as string, soy, lima, green, and snap
- Peas
- Potatoes
- Arrowroot flour
- Grains such as flax, millet, quinoa, and amaranth
- Nuts like almonds, pignoli, fresh coconut, and chestnuts
- Sprouted seeds of alfalfa, radish, and chia
- Unsprouted sesame
- Fresh unsalted butter
- Whey
- Plain yogurt
- Fruit juices
- All vegetable juices
- Most herbal teas

- Garlic
- Cayenne pepper
- Gelatin
- Most herbs
- Miso
- Most vegetable and unprocessed sea salt
- Most all spices
- Vanilla extract
- Sweeteners like raw, unpasteurized honey, dried sugar cane juice (Sucanat), brown rice syrup
- Brewer's yeast

Chapter 3
What Can and Can not Be Affected by What You Eat
Understanding the Difference between Blood pH, Saliva pH, and Urine pH

Blood pH:

Blood pH indicates the acidity of the blood. Its normal value ranges from 7.35 to 7.45. A level greater and lower than this can cause serious health problems.

Urine pH

The urine pH indicates the level of acidity in the urine released out of the body. Lower pH value states the urine is more acidic, which is the sign of possible future kidney stones and accumulation of uric acid. The normal pH value for urine ranges from 6 to 7.5. Any value lower than this should be treated before it may lead to diarrhea, acidosis, or diabetic ketoacidosis.

Saliva pH:

Digestion of food starts right from the mouth when the food is mixed with saliva, carrying enzymes. This saliva has a normal pH of 5.6 to 7.9. Thus, it is termed as neutral to slightly alkaline.

Testing Urine and Salvia pH

pH testing strips are available online and in the market which can instantly detect the pH level of both the saliva and the urine. Both can be tested through different procedures.

Urine test:

Check the pH of urine right in the morning before drinking or eating anything.

Lightly wet the pH test strips with the urine for 2 seconds and then match the appeared color with the given labels.

Saliva Test:

For saliva, test strips are also available which indicates the pH level through changing colors. Never put the strips directly into the mouth. Rather slightly dap the strip with some saliva and leave it for 2 seconds.

Do not test directly after eating or drinking anything. Wait for 30 minutes and then check the pH of your saliva.

The 80/20 Rule

This rule states that for a diet to be termed as alkaline, it must contain 80 percent alkaline forming food and 20 percent acid forming food. The rule helps most of the beginners, as it gives a clear-cut outline and a standard measure to pass every food item through a general alkaline diet meter.

Acid-Forming Foods to Avoid

As already discussed above, alkaline diet prohibits all the acid forming food items. Therefore, all such products should be avoided. These includes:

- All types of meat including seafood
- Rice of all types
- Bread and market bought crackers.
- Pasta
- Beans
- Artificial sweeteners
- Acidic Vegetables like lemons or limes
- Oatmeal, oats, cornmeal, etc
- Dairy products

Fermented foods and their role

Fermentation is described as the process of breaking down sugars by bacteria releasing energy. Fermented foods are rich in microbes and probiotics. They help the gut bacteria to maintain the alkaline environment and aid the digestion process .Fermented items include miso, tempeh, sauerkraut, and kefir, etc. The benefits of fermented food are as follows.

1. Better digestion.

2. Providing more gut bacteria

3. Easier to preserve and long-lasting.

Acid-Forming Foods to Avoid

Following is the list of items which are prescribed on an alkaline diet:

Vegetables	Fruits	Nuts and Spices	Oils and Dairy	Beverages	Bread and grains
Asparagus	Blackberries	Chestnuts	Ghee	Mineral water	Oatmeal
Celery	Strawberries	Sea Salt	Olive oil	Ginger tea	Apple crisp
Artichokes	Raspberries	Ginger Root	Avocado oil	Grapefruit juice	Granola
Collard greens	Cantaloupe	Pumpkin Seeds	Coconut Oil	Apple Juice	
Kale	Watermelon	Black pepper	Cod liver oil	Pineapple Juice	
Endive	Raisins	Cashews		Grape juice	
Sweet potatoes	Blueberries	Garlic		Green tea	
Potato	Apples	Almonds			
Bell	Apricots	Cinnamo			

peppers		n			
Broccoli	Avocado	Soy sauce			
Cabbage	Banana				
Carrots					
Snow peas					
Cucumbers					
Cauliflower					
Brussels sprout					

BREAKFAST RECIPES

Crunchy Quinoa Meal

Ingredients:

- 3 cups almond milk
- 1 cup quinoa, rinsed
- 1/8 teaspoon ground cinnamon
- 1 cup raspberry
- ½ cup choppedchopped almonds

How to prepare:

1. Add milk into a saucepan and bring to a boil over high heat.

2. Add quinoa to the milk and again bring it to a boil.
3. Let it simmer for 15 minutes, on low heat until milk is reduced.
4. Stir in cinnamon and mix well.
5. Cover and cook for 8 minutes until milk is completely absorbed.
6. Add raspberry and cook for 30 seconds.
7. Serve and enjoy.

Preparation time: 5 minutes
Cooking time: 25 minutes
Total time: 30 minutes
Servings: 2

Nutritional Values:

- *Calories 271*
- *Total Fat 3.7 g*
- *Saturated Fat 2.7 g*
- *Cholesterol 168 mg*
- *Sodium 121 mg*
- *Total Carbs 54 g*
- *Fiber 3.5 g*
- *Sugar 2.3 g*
- *Protein 6.5 g*

Almond Pancakes

Ingredients:

- 1 cup almond flour
- 2 tablespoons arrowroot powder
- 1 teaspoon baking powder
- 1 cup almond milk
- 3 tablespoons coconut oil

How to prepare:

1. Mix all dry ingredients in a medium container.
2. Add almond milk and 2 tablespoons coconut oil. Mix well.
3. Melt a teaspoon coconut oil in a skillet.
4. Pour a ladle of the batter into the skillet and swirl the pan to spread it into a smooth pancake.

5. Cook for 3 minutes on low heat until firm.

6. Flip the pancake and cook for another 2 to 3 minutes until golden brown.

7. Cook more pancakes using the remaining batter.

8. Serve.

Preparation time: 5 minutes

Cooking time: 15 minutes

Total time: 20 minutes

Servings: 4

Nutritional Values:

- *Calories 377*
- *Total Fat 14.9 g*
- *Saturated Fat 4.7 g*
- *Cholesterol 194 mg*
- *Sodium 607 mg*
- *Total Carbs 60.7 g*
- *Fiber 1.4 g*
- *Sugar 3.3 g*
- *Protein 6.4g*

Quinoa Porridge

Ingredients:

- 2 cups almond milk
- 1 cup quinoa, rinsed
- 1/8 teaspoon ground cinnamon
- 1 cup (1/2 pint) fresh blueberries

How to prepare:

1. Boil almond milk in a saucepan over high heat.
2. Add quinoa to the milk and again bring it to a boil.
3. Let it simmer for 15 minutes on low heat until milk is reduced.
4. Stir in cinnamon and mix well.
5. Cover and cook for 8 mins until milk is completely absorbed.

6. Add blueberries and cook for 30 seconds.

7. Serve and enjoy.

Preparation time: 5 minutes

Cooking time: 25 minutes

Total time: 30 minutes

Servings: 2

Nutritional Values:

- Calories 271
- Total Fat 3.7 g
- Saturated Fat 2.7 g
- Cholesterol 168 mg
- Sodium 121 mg
- Total Carbs 54 g
- Fiber 3.5 g
- Sugar 2.3 g
- Protein 6.5

Amaranth Porridge

Ingredients:

- 2 cups almond milk
- 2 cups alkaline water
- 1 cup amaranth
- 2 tablespoons coconut oil
- 1 tablespoon ground cinnamon

How to prepare:

1. Mix milk with water in a medium saucepan.
2. Bring the mixture to a boil.
3. Stir in amaranth then reduce the heat to low.
4. Cook on low simmer for 30 minutes with occasional stirring.
5. Turn off the heat. Stir in cinnamon and coconut oil.
6. Serve warm.

Preparation time: 05 minutes

Cooking time: 30 minutes

Total time: 35 minutes

Servings: 2

Nutritional Values:

- Calories 434
- Total Fat 35 g
- Saturated Fat 0 g
- Cholesterol 0 mg
- Sodium 3 mg
- Total Carbs 27 g
- Fiber 3.6 g
- Sugar 5.5 g
- Protein 6.7

Banana Barley Porridge

Ingredients:

- 1 cup unsweetened almond milk, divided
- 1 small banana, peeled and sliced
- ½ cup barley
- 3 drops liquid stevia
- ¼ cup almonds, choppedchopped

Method:

1. Mix barley with half almond milk and stevia in a bowl and mix well.
2. Cover and refrigerate for about 6 hours.
3. Mix the barley mixture with almond milk in a saucepan.
4. Cook for 5 minutes on medium heat.

5. Top with choppedchopped almonds and banana slices.
6. Serve.

Preparation Time: 15 minutes

Cooking Time: 5 minutes

Total Time: 20 minutes

Servings: 2

Nutritional Value:

- Calories 159
- Total Fat 8.4 g
- Saturated Fat 0.7 g
- Cholesterol 0 mg
- Total Carbs 19.8 g
- Dietary Fiber 4.1 g
- Sugar 6.7 g
- Protein *4.6 g*

Zucchini Muffins

Ingredients:

- 1 tablespoon ground flaxseed
- 3 tablespoons alkaline water
- ¼ cup almond butter
- 3 small-medium over-ripe bananas
- 2 small zucchinis, grated
- ½ cup almond milk
- 1 teaspoon vanilla extract
- 2 cups almond flour
- 1 tablespoon baking powder
- 1 teaspoon cinnamon
- ¼ teaspoon sea salt

Optional addins:

- ¼ cup chocolate chips and/or walnuts

How to prepare:

1. Set your oven to 375 degrees F. Grease a muffin tray with cooking spray.
2. Mix flaxseed with water in a bowl.
3. Mash bananas in a glass bowl and stir in all the remaining ingredients.
4. Mix well and divide the mixture into the muffin tray.
5. Bake for 25 minutes.
6. Serve.

Preparation time: 10 minutes
Cooking time: 25 minutes
Total time: 35 minutes
Servings: 16

Nutritional Values:

- *Calories 127*
- *Total Fat 6.6 g*
- *Saturated Fat 1.1 g*
- *Cholesterol 0 mg*
- *Sodium 292 mg*
- *Total Carbs 13 g*
- *Fiber 0.7 g*
- *Sugar 1.2 g*
- *Protein 3.8 g*

Millet Porridge

Ingredients:

- Pinch of sea salt
- 1 tablespoon almonds, choppedchopped finely
- ½ cup unsweetened almond milk
- ½ cup millet, rinsed and drained
- 1½ cups alkaline water
- 3 drops liquid stevia

Method:

1. Sauté millet in a non-stick skillet for 3 minutes.
2. Stir in salt and water. Let it boil then reduce the heat.
3. Cook for 15 minutes then stirs in remaining ingredients.

4. Cook for another 4 minutes.

5. Serve with choppedchopped nuts on top.

Preparation Time: 10 minutes

Cooking Time: 20 minutes

Total Time: 30 minutes

Servings: 2

Nutritional Value:

- Calories 219
- Total Fat 4.5 g
- Saturated Fat 0.6 g
- Cholesterol 0 mg
- Total Carbs 38.2 g
- Fiber 5 g
- Sugar 0.6 g
- Protein *6.4 g*

Tofu Vegetable Fry

Ingredients:

- 2 small onions, finely choppedchopped
- 2 cups cherry tomatoes, finely choppedchopped
- 1/8 teaspoon ground turmeric
- 1 tablespoon olive oil
- 2 red bell peppers, seeded and choppedchopped
- 3 cups firm tofu, crumbled and choppedchopped
- 1/8 teaspoon cayenne pepper
- 2 tablespoons fresh basil leaves, choppedchopped
- Salt, to taste

Method:

1. Sauté onions and bell peppers in a greased skillet for 5 minutes.
2. Stir in tomatoes and cook for 2 minutes.
3. Add turmeric, salt, cayenne pepper, and tofu.
4. Cook for 8 minutes.
5. Garnish with basil leaves.
6. Serve warm.

Preparation Time: 10 minutes
Cooking Time: 15 minutes
Total Time: 25 minutes
Servings: 4

Nutritional Value:

- Calories 212
- Total Fat 11.8 g
- Saturated Fat 2.2 g
- Cholesterol 0 mg
- Total Carbs 14.6 g
- Dietary Fiber 4.4 g
- Sugar 8 g
- Protein *17.3 g*

Zucchini Pancakes

Ingredients:

- 12 tablespoons alkaline water

- 6 large zucchinis, grated

- Sea salt, to taste

- 4 tablespoons ground Flax Seeds

- 2 teaspoons olive oil

- 2 jalapeño peppers, finely choppedchopped

- ½ cup scallions, finely choppedchopped

Method:

1. Mix together water and flax seeds in a bowl and keep aside.

2. Heat oil in a large non-stick skillet on medium heat and add zucchini, salt, and black pepper.
3. Cook for about 3 minutes and transfer the zucchini into a large bowl.
4. Stir in scallions and flax seed mixture and thoroughly mix.
5. Preheat a griddle and grease it lightly with cooking spray.
6. Pour about ¼ of the zucchini mixture into preheated griddle and cook for about 3 minutes.
7. Flip the side carefully and cook for about 2 more minutes.
8. Repeat with the remaining mixture in batches and serve.

Preparation Time: 15 minutes
Cooking Time: 8 minutes
Total Time: 23 minutes
Servings: 8

Nutritional Value:
- Calories 71
- Total Fat 2.8 g
- Saturated Fat 0.4 g
- Cholesterol 0 mg
- Total Carbs 9.8 g
- Dietary Fiber 3.9 g
- Sugar 4.5 g
- Protein *3.7 g*

Pumpkin Spice Quinoa

Ingredients:

- 1 cup cooked quinoa
- 1 cup unsweetened almond milk
- 1 large banana, mashed
- 1/4 cup pumpkin puree
- 1 teaspoon pumpkin spice
- 2 teaspoon chia seeds

How to prepare:

1. Mix all the ingredients in a container.
2. Seal the lid and shake well to mix.
3. Refrigerate overnight.
4. Serve.

Preparation time: 10 minutes

Cooking time: 0minutes

Total time: 10 minutes

Servings: 02

Nutritional Value:

- *Calories 212*
- *Total Fat 11.9 g*
- *Saturated Fat 02 g*
- *Cholesterol 112 mg*
- *Sodium 125 mg*
- *Total Carbs 31.7 g*
- *Fiber 2 g*
- *Sugar 2.3 g*
- *Protein 7.3g*

SMOOTHIE RECIPES

Apple Ginger Smoothie

Ingredients:

- 1 Apple, peeled and diced
- ¾ cup (6 oz) coconut yogurt
- ½ teaspoon ginger, freshly grated

How to prepare:

1. Add all the ingredients to a blender.
2. Blend well until smooth.
3. Refrigerate for 2 to 3 hours.
4. Serve.

Preparation time: 10 minutes

Cooking time: 0 minutes

Total time: 10 minutes

Servings: 01

Nutritional Values:

- *Calories 144*
- *Total Fat 0.4 g*
- *Saturated Fat 5 g*
- *Cholesterol 51 mg*
- *Sodium 86 mg*
- *Total Carbs 8 g*
- *Fiber 2.3 g*
- *Sugar 2.2 g*
- *Protein 5.6 g*

Green Tea Blueberry Smoothie

Ingredients:

- 3 tablespoons alkaline water
- 1 green tea bag
- 1½ cup fresh blueberries
- 1 pear, peeled, cored and diced
- ¾ cup almond milk

How to prepare:

1. Boil 3 tablespoons water in a small pot and transfer it to a cup.
2. Dip the tea bag in the cup and let it sit for 4 to 5 mins.
3. Discard tea bag and
4. Transfer the green tea to a blender

5. Add all the remaining the ingredients to the blender.

6. Blend well until smooth.

7. Serve with fresh blueberries.

Preparation time: 10 minutes

Cooking time: 5 minutes

Total time: 15 minutes

Servings: 01

Nutritional Values:

- *Calories 144*
- *Total Fat 0.4 g*
- *Saturated Fat 5 g*
- *Cholesterol 51 mg*
- *Sodium 86 mg*
- *Total Carbs 8 g*
- *Fiber 2.3 g*
- *Sugar 2.2 g*
- *Protein 5.6 g*

Apple Almond Smoothie

Ingredients:

- 1 cup apple cider
- 1/2 cup coconut yogurt
- 4 tablespoons almonds, crushed
- 1/4 teaspoon cinnamon
- 1/4 teaspoon nutmeg
- 1 cup ice cubes

How to prepare:

1. Add all the ingredients to a blender.
2. Blend well until smooth.
3. Serve.

Preparation time: 10 minutes

Cooking time: 0 minutes

Total time: 10 minutes

Servings: 01

Nutritional Values:

- Calories 144
- Total Fat 0.4 g
- Saturated Fat 5 g
- Cholesterol 51 mg
- Sodium 86 mg
- Total Carbs 8 g
- Fiber 2.3 g
- Sugar 2.2 g
- Protein 5.6 *g*

Cranberry Smoothie

Ingredients:

- 1 cup cranberries
- ¾ cup almond milk
- ¼ cup raspberries
- 2 teaspoon fresh ginger, finely grated
- 2 teaspoons fresh lemon juice

How to prepare:

1. Add all the ingredients to a blender.
2. Blend well until smooth.
3. Serve with fresh berries on top.

Preparation time: 10 minutes
Cooking time: 0 minutes

Total time: 10 minutes

Servings: 01

Nutritional Values:

- *Calories 144*
- *Total Fat 0.4 g*
- *Saturated Fat 5 g*
- *Cholesterol 51 mg*
- *Sodium 86 mg*
- *Total Carbs 8 g*
- *Fiber 2.3 g*
- *Sugar 2.2 g*
- *Protein 5.6* g

Cinnamon Berry Smoothie

Ingredients:

- 1 cup frozen strawberries
- 1 cup apple, peeled and diced
- 2 teaspoon fresh ginger
- 3 tablespoons hemp seeds
- 1 cup water
- ½ lime juiced
- ¼ teaspoon cinnamon powder
- ⅛ teaspoon vanilla extract

How to prepare:

1. Add all the ingredients to a blender.
2. Blend well until smooth.
3. Serve with fresh fruits

Preparation time: 10 minutes

Cooking time: 0 minutes

Total time: 10 minutes

Servings: 01

Nutritional Values:

- *Calories 144*
- *Total Fat 0.4 g*
- *Saturated Fat 5 g*
- *Cholesterol 51 mg*
- *Sodium 86 mg*
- *Total Carbs 8 g*
- *Fiber 2.3 g*
- *Sugar 2.2 g*
- *Protein 5.6 g*

Detox Berries smoothie

Ingredients:

- 3 peaches, cored and peeled
- 5 blueberries
- 5 raspberries
- 1 cup alkaline water

How to prepare:

1. Add all the ingredients to a blender.
2. Blend well until smooth.
3. Serve with fresh kiwi wedges.

Preparation time: 10 minutes

Cooking time: 0 minutes

Total time: 10 minutes

Servings: 01

Nutritional Values:

- *Calories 144*
- *Total Fat 0.4 g*
- *Saturated Fat 5 g*
- *Cholesterol 51 mg*
- *Sodium 86 mg*
- *Total Carbs 8 g*
- *Fiber 2.3 g*
- *Sugar 2.2 g*
- *Protein 5.6 g*

Pink Smoothie

Ingredients:

- 1 peach, cored and peeled
- 6 ripe strawberries
- 1 cup almond milk

How to prepare:

1. Add all the ingredients to a blender.
2. Blend well until smooth.
3. Serve with your favorite berries

Preparation time: 10 minutes

Cooking time: 0 minutes

Total time: 10 minutes

Servings: 01

Nutritional Values:

- *Calories 144*
- *Total Fat 0.4 g*
- *Saturated Fat 5 g*
- *Cholesterol 51 mg*
- *Sodium 86 mg*
- *Total Carbs 8 g*
- *Fiber 2.3 g*
- *Sugar 2.2 g*
- *Protein 5.6 g*

Green Apple Smoothie

Ingredients:

- 1 peach , peeled and cored
- 1 green apple, peeled and cored
- 1 cup alkaline water

How to prepare:

1. Add all the ingredients to a blender.
2. Blend well until smooth.
3. Serve with apple slices.

Preparation time: 10 minutes
Cooking time: 0 minutes
Total time: 10 minutes
Servings: 01

Nutritional Values:

- *Calories 144*
- *Total Fat 0.4 g*
- *Saturated Fat 5 g*
- *Cholesterol 51 mg*
- *Sodium 86 mg*
- *Total Carbs 8 g*
- *Fiber 2.3 g*
- *Sugar 2.2 g*
- *Protein 5.6* g

Avocado Smoothie

Ingredients:

- *1 carrot, grated*
- *1 avocado, cored and peeled*
- *½ pear, cored*
- *½ cup blackberries*
- *1 ½ cups unsweetened almond milk*

How to prepare:

1. Add all the ingredients to a blender.
2. Blend well until smooth.
3. Serve with blackberries on top.

Preparation time: 10 minutes
Cooking time: 0 minutes

Total time: 10 minutes

Servings: 01

Nutritional Values:

- *Calories 144*
- *Total Fat 0.4 g*
- *Saturated Fat 5 g*
- *Cholesterol 51 mg*
- *Sodium 86 mg*
- *Total Carbs 8 g*
- *Fiber 2.3 g*
- *Sugar 2.2 g*
- *Protein 5.6 g*

Green Smoothie

Ingredients:

- 1 cup alkaline water
- 3/4 cup raw coconut water
- 1/2 teaspoon probiotic powder
- 2 cups firmly packed baby spinach
- 1 cup raw young Thai coconut meat
- 1 avocado, peeled and pitted
- 1/2 cucumber, choppedchopped
- 1 teaspoon lime zest, finely grated
- 2 limes, hav
- led
- Stevia, to taste

- *Pinch of Celtic sea salt*
- *2 cups ice cubes*

How to prepare:

1. Add all the ingredients to a blender.
2. Blend well until smooth.
3. Serve with an avocado slice on top.

Preparation time: 10 minutes

Cooking time: 0 minutes

Total time: 10 minutes

Servings: 01

Nutritional Values:

- *Calories 144*
- *Total Fat 0.4 g*
- *Saturated Fat 5 g*
- *Cholesterol 51 mg*
- *Sodium 86 mg*
- *Total Carbs 8 g*
- *Fiber 2.3 g*
- *Sugar 2.2 g*
- *Protein 5.6 g*

LUNCH RECIPES

Sprout Onion Fry

Ingredients:

- 2½ pounds Brussels sprouts, trimmed4 slices bacon, cut into 1-inch pieces
- 1 tablespoon extra-virgin coconut oil
- 1 tomato, choppedchopped
- 1 onion, choppedchopped
- 4 sprigs thyme or savory, divided
- 1 teaspoon Celtic sea salt, iodine free
- Freshly ground pepper to taste
- 2 teaspoons lemon juice (optional)

How to prepare:

1. *Add sprouts to the boiling water in a stockpot.*
2. *Let them cook for about3 to 5 minutes.*
3. *Drain and set them aside.*
4. *Saute onions in a greased skillet for 4 minutes.*
5. *Stir in salt, pepper, and thyme*
6. *Add drained sprouts to the skillet and stir cook for 3 minutes.*
7. *Remove and discard the herb sprigs.*
8. *Serve warm with lemon juice and choppedchopped spring onion on top.*

Preparation time: 5 minutes
Cooking time: 10 minutes
Total time: 15 minutes
Servings: 04

Nutritional Values:

- *Calories 383*
- *Total Fat 5.3 g*
- *Saturated Fat 3.9 g*
- *Cholesterol 135 mg*
- *Sodium 487 mg*
- *Total Carbs 76.8 g*
- *Fibre 0.1g*
- *Sugar 0 g*
- *Protein 27.7 g*

Veggies with Mushrooms

Ingredients:

- 1 teaspoon coconut oil
- 1 cup mushroom, sliced
- ½ cup onion, choppedchopped
- 2 tablespoons garlic, smashed
- 2 tablespoons ginger, finely choppedchopped
- 1 ½ tablespoons sambal oelek
- 1 ½ cups cabbage, choppedchopped
- 2 cups leeks, white part only,choppedchopped
- ½ cup celery, choppedchopped
- 2 tablespoons jalapenos, sliced
- ¼ cup green bell peppers , sliced
- 3 tablespoons vegetable stock

How to prepare:

1. Sauté mushrooms and onion in a greased skillet for 3 minutes.
2. Stir in ginger, garlic, Sambal Oelek and sauté for 30 seconds.
3. Add cabbage, leeks, peppers and cook for 2 minutes.
4. Adjust seasoning with salt and pepper.
5. Add vegetable stock and cook for 1 minute.
6. Serve warm.

Preparation time: 5 minutes

Cooking time: 10 minutes

Total time: 15 minutes

Servings: 4

Nutritional Values:

- *Calories 398*
- *Total Fat 13.8 g*
- *Saturated Fat 5.1 g*
- *Cholesterol 200 mg*
- *Sodium 272 mg*
- *Total Carbs 13.6 g*
- *Fiber 1 g*
- *Sugar 1.3 g*
- *Protein 51.8 g*

Green Bean Stir Fry

Ingredients:

- 2 tablespoons unseasoned rice vinegar
- 1 lb. green beans, trimmed and cut into pieces
- 1 tablespoon grapeseed oil
- 1 teaspoon red pepper flakes
- Celtic sea salt, iodine free
- 2 garlic cloves, crushed
- Freshly ground black pepper, to taste
- 2 tablespoons coconut oil
- 1-inch piece ginger, minced

How to prepare:

1. Add coconut oil and green bean to the skillet and sauté for 2 to 3 minutes.

2. Stir in ginger and garlic. Cook for 2 minutes.

3. Add all the remaining ingredients.

4. Serve warm.

Preparation time: 10 minutes

Cooking time: 10 minutes

Total time: 20 minutes

Servings: 2

Nutritional Values:

- *Calories 372*
- *Total Fat 11.8 g*
- *Saturated Fat 4.4 g*
- *Cholesterol 62 mg*
- *Sodium 1871 mg*
- *Total Carbs 31.8 g*
- *Fiber 0.6 g*
- *Sugar 27.3 g*
- *Protein 34 g*

Rosemary Roasted Yams

Ingredients:

- 2 cups cubed yams
- 1 tablespoon coconut oil
- 6 fresh rosemary sprigs leave removed and finely choppedchopped stems discarded
- Celtic sea salt, iodine free, to taste
- Black pepper to taste

How to prepare:

1. Preheat your oven to 375 degrees F.
2. Mix yams with rosemary and oil in a bowl.
3. Spread the yams on a baking sheet.
4. Bake for 45 to 50 minutes.

5. Adjust seasoning with salt and pepper.

6. Serve warm.

Preparation time: 10 minutes

Cooking time: 45 minutes

Total time: 55 minutes

Servings: 4

Nutritional Values:

- *Calories 341*
- *Total Fat 34 g*
- *Saturated Fat 8.5 g*
- *Cholesterol 69 mg*
- *Sodium 547 mg*
- *Total Carbs 36.4 g*
- *Fiber 1.2 g*
- *Sugar 1 g*
- *Protein 20.3 g*

Peach Panzanella

Ingredients:

- 3 shallots, finely sliced into rings
- 2 tablespoons cider vinegar
- 3 firm peaches, halved
- 3 ½ tablespoons coconut oil
- 1 pinch of red chili flakes
- 1 pinch of fennel seeds
- Juice ½ lemon
- 1 handful wild rocket small pack basil , leaves picked
- 1 cup cherry tomatoes, halved

How to prepare:

1. Toss peaches with coconut oil, fennel seeds, chili flakes, and seasoning in a bowl.
2. Heat a pan over high heat and add peaches to cook for 2 minutes per side.
3. Place the peaches in a plate. Set them aside.
4. Mix shallots with vinegar, coconut oil, and seasoning in a bowl.
5. Stir in capers, basil, and tomato and lemon juice.
6. Toss in peaches.
7. Serve.

Preparation time: 10 minutes
Cooking time: 05 minutes
Total time: 15 minutes
Servings: 02

Nutritional Values:

- *Calories 311*
- *Total Fat 25.5 g*
- *Saturated Fat 12.4 g*
- *Cholesterol 69 mg*
- *Sodium 58 mg*
- *Total Carbs 1.4 g*
- *Fiber 0.7 g*
- *Sugar 0.3 g*
- *Protein 18.4 g*

Cabbage with Coconut & Sweet Potato

Ingredients:

- 1 lb. sweet potatoes, unpeeled and halved
- 2 tablespoons coconut oil
- 1 pinch Asafoetida
- 1 teaspoon black mustard seeds
- 1 teaspoon cumin seeds
- 2 dried red chilies
- 1 fresh red or green chili, seeds removed and thinly sliced
- 1 head cabbage, finely shredded
- Juice ½ lemon
- 2 tablespoons desiccated or shaved fresh coconut

How to prepare:

1. Add water with salt to a large pot and boil it.
2. Stir in potatoes and cook for 10 minutes.
3. Drain and transfer them to a bowl. Crush them with a fork gently (do not mash)
4. Heat oil in a large skillet and add spices, Asafoetida, and chilies.
5. Sauté for 2 mins and toss in cabbage, fresh chili, and salt.
6. Stir cook about 3 to 4 minutes.
7. Stir in drained potatoes and cook for 2 to 3 minutes.
8. Add coconut, coriander, and lemon juice
9. Mix well and serve warm with coconut yogurt.

Preparation time: 10 minutes
Cooking time: 10 minutes
Total time: 20 minutes
Servings: 2

Nutritional Values:

- *Calories 604*
- *Total Fat 30.6 g*
- *Saturated Fat 13.1 g*
- *Cholesterol 131 mg*
- *Sodium 1834 mg*
- *Total Carbs 21.4g*
- *Fiber 0.2 g*
- *Sugar 20.3 g*
- *Protein 54.6 g*

Cauliflower Curry Soup

Ingredients:

- 1 large head of cauliflower, choppedchopped
- 4 tablespoons coconut oil, divided
- 1 medium yellow onion, diced
- 2 to 3 tablespoons Thai red curry paste
- ½ teaspoon lemon zest
- ½ cup unoaked white wine
- 1 ½ cups vegetable stock
- 1 can (14 ounces) light coconut milk
- 1 to 3 teaspoons rice vinegar
- Celtic sea salt, iodine free, to taste
- Freshly ground black pepper, to taste

- 1 tablespoon choppedchopped fresh basil
- Nuts to garnish

How to prepare:

1. Preheat your oven to 400 degrees F.
2. Mix cauliflower with coconut oil in a bowl.
3. Spread it on a large baking sheet. Bake for about 25 to 30 minutes.
4. Melt a tablespoon coconut oil in a Dutch oven.
5. Add onion with a dash of salt to sauté for 3 minutes.
6. Stir in curry paste and lemon zest.
7. Mix well then add wine and cook until it is completely absorbed
8. Add roasted cauliflower, coconut milk, and vegetable stock.
9. Let it cook for 10 minutes on low simmer.
10. Puree the soup using a handheld blender after cooling for 5 minutes.
11. Adjust seasoning with salt and pepper.
12. Garnish with basil and nuts.
13. Serve warm.

Preparation time: 10 minutes

Cooking time: 45 minutes

Total time: 55 minutes

Servings: 04

Nutritional Values:

- *Calories 338*
- *Total Fat 3.8 g*
- *Saturated Fat 0.7 g*
- *Cholesterol 22 mg*
- *Sodium 620 mg*
- *Total Carbs 58.3 g*
- *Fiber 2.4 g*
- *Sugar 1.2 g*
- *Protein 15.4g*

Carrot Sweet Potato Soup

Ingredients:

- 1 tablespoon coconut oil
- 2 cups yellow onion, choppedchopped
- 2 cloves garlic, minced
- 1 tablespoon fresh ginger, minced
- 2 tablespoons red curry paste
- 4 cups low-sodium vegetable broth
- 3 cups diced carrots, peeled
- 3 cups sweet potatoes, peeled and diced
- Celtic sea salt, iodine free, to taste
- Freshly ground black pepper to taste
- ¼ teaspoon cayenne pepper

How to prepare:

1. Sauté garlic, onion, and ginger in a greased pan for 5 to 6 minutes.
2. Stir in curry paste and broth.
3. Mix well then add carrots, salt, and sweet potatoes
4. Boil the soup on high heat.
5. Cover the pot. Cook for 15 to 20 minutes.
6. Blend this soup in a blender in batches until smooth.
7. Adjust seasoning with salt and pepper.
8. Divide the soup into the serving bowl.
9. Serve warm.

Preparation time: 10 minutes
Cooking time: 30 minutes
Total time: 40 minutes
Servings: 04

Nutritional Values:

- *Calories 338*
- *Total Fat 3.8 g*
- *Saturated Fat 0.7 g*
- *Cholesterol 22 mg*
- *Sodium 620 mg*
- *Total Carbs 58.3 g*
- *Fiber 2.4 g*
- *Sugar 1.2 g*
- *Protein 15.4g*

Ingredients:

- 3 tablespoons coconut oil
- 1 medium yellow or white onion, choppedchopped
- 3 carrots, peeled and choppedchopped
- 2 celery stalks, choppedchopped
- 1 cup zucchini or any seasonal vegetable
- 6 garlic cloves, pressed or minced
- ½ teaspoon dried thyme
- 1 can (28 ounces) diced tomatoes, drained
- 1 cup quinoa, rinsed and drained
- 4 cups vegetable broth
- 2 cups alkaline water

- 1 teaspoon Celtic sea salt, iodine free, or more to taste
- 2 bay leaves
- Pinch red pepper flakes
- Freshly ground black pepper, to taste
- 1 teaspoon lemon juice

How to prepare:

1. Add oil to a stock pot and heat it over medium heat.
2. Add onion, celery, carrots, salt, and zucchini to the oil.
3. Sauté for about 6 to 8 minutes.
4. Stir in thyme and garlic and sauté for 1 minute.
5. Add drained tomatoes and cook for 5 to 6 minutes.
6. Pour in broth, water, and quinoa.
7. Stir in red pepper flakes, bay leaves and salt.
8. Bring the mixture to a boil then reduce the heat.
9. Partially cover the lid and let it simmer for 25 minutes.
10. Turn off the pot heat and discard the bay leaves.
11. Add lemon juice, salt, and pepper.
12. Serve warm.

Preparation time: 10 minutes

Cooking time: 45 minutes

Total time: 55 minutes

Servings: 04

Nutritional Values:

- *Calories 336*
- *Total Fat 14.8 g*
- *Saturated Fat 0.7 g*
- *Cholesterol 22 mg*
- *Sodium 620 mg*
- *Total Carbs 40.3 g*
- *Fiber 2.4 g*
- *Sugar 1.2 g*
- *Protein 12.4g*

Zucchini Lasagna

Ingredients:

- Basil-Cashew Cheese
- 1 cup unsalted cashews, soaked and drained
- ½ cup unsweetened almond milk
- ¼ cup fresh basil leaves
- 2 garlic cloves
- ½ teaspoon sea salt

Artichoke-Tomato Sauce

- 1 tablespoon olive oil
- 1 onion, diced
- 2 garlic cloves, minced
- 14.5-ounce diced tomatoes
- 8-ounce tomato sauce

- 1 cup artichoke hearts, choppedchopped
- ¼ cup fresh basil leaves, torn into pieces
- Red pepper flakes, to taste
- Sea salt, to taste
- Freshly ground black pepper, to taste
- Zucchini Lasagna
- 6 medium zucchinis, thinly sliced
- Sea salt
- Fresh basil, for garnish
- Olive oil, for drizzling
- Basil Cheese

How to prepare:

1. Blend all the ingredients in a blender.
2. Saute onions in a greased pan for 3 minutes.
3. Add garlic and sauté for 30 seconds.
4. Stir tomato sauce, tomatoes, artichoke, and basil.
5. Adjust seasoning with salt, pepper, and flakes.
6. Boil the mixture then reduce the heat to a simmer. Cook for 10 minutes.
7. Preheat your oven to 375 degrees F.
8. Spread tomato sauce at the base of a casserole dish.
9. Top it with a layer of zucchini slices.
10. Add another layer of tomato sauce and cashew cheese.

11. Repeat the layers ending with the top layer of sauce and cheese.
12. Garnish with olive oil and basil.
13. Cover the casserole dish and bake for 30 minutes.
14. Uncover and bake for another 25 minutes.
15. Allow it to rest for 15 minutes.
16. Slice and serve.

Preparation time: 10 minutes
Cooking time: 1 hr. 30 minutes
Total time: 1 hr. 40 minutes
Servings: 06

Nutritional Values:
- *Calories 338*
- *Total Fat 3.8 g*
- *Saturated Fat 0.7 g*
- *Cholesterol 22 mg*
- *Sodium 620 mg*
- *Total Carbs 58.3 g*
- *Fiber 2.4 g*
- *Sugar 1.2 g*
- *Protein 15.4g*

DINNER RECIPES

Carrot and Golden Beet Soup

Ingredients:

- 6-7 carrots, choppedchopped into 1/2 inch pieces
- 2-3 golden beets, choppedchopped into 1/2 inch cubes
- 2 shallots, choppedchopped into chunks
- 1 tablespoon olive oil
- 1/4 teaspoons ground turmeric, divided
- 1/4 teaspoons ground cumin, divided
- 1/2 teaspoons dried thyme, divided
- 1/2 teaspoons sea salt
- 2-3 cups vegetable stock
- 2-3 teaspoons lime juice

For serving

- Chopped cilantro or parsley for serving, optional

How to prepare:
1. Layer 2 baking sheets with tin foil. Preheat the oven to 400 degrees F.
2. Add carrots, beet, and shallot to the baking sheets.
3. Top the veggies with spices, salt, and herbs.
4. Drizzle half tablespoon oil and cover the veggies with a foil sheet.
5. Bake for 30 minutes until al dente.
6. Transfer all the ingredients to a blender.
7. Puree the mixture and add the saucepan.
8. Cook for 1 minute.
9. Garnish with parsley.
10. Serve.

Preparation time: 5 minutes
Cooking time: 30 minutes
Total time: 35 minutes
Servings: 04

Nutritional Values:
- *Calories 248*
- *Total Fat 15.7 g*
- *Saturated Fat 2.7 g*
- *Cholesterol 75 mg*
- *Sodium 94 mg*
- *Total Carbs 0.4 g*
- *Fibre 0g*
- *Sugar 0 g*
- *Protein 24.9 g*

Sweet Potato Green Soup

Ingredients:

- 2 tablespoons coconut oil
- 1 large onion, choppedchopped
- 3 cloves garlic, minced
- 2-in piece ginger, peeled and minced
- 3 cups bone broth
- 1 medium white sweet potato, cubed
- 1 large head broccoli, choppedchopped
- 1 bunch kale, choppedchopped
- 1 lemon, ½ zested and juice reserved
- ½ teaspoon sea salt
- 1 bunch cilantro

How to prepare:

1. Add and heat oil in a skillet. Stir in onions.
2. Sauté for 7 minutes then add ginger and garlic. Cook for 1 minute.
3. Stir in sweet potato, broccoli, and broth.
4. Boil the soup then reduce the heat to a simmer.
5. Cook for 15 minutes then turn off the heat.
6. Add all the remaining ingredients.
7. Puree the mixture using a handheld blender.
8. Garnish with cilantro.
9. Serve warm.

Preparation time: 5 minutes
Cooking time: 22 minutes
Total time: 27 minutes
Servings: 2

Nutritional Values:

- *Calories 249*
- *Total Fat 11.9 g*
- *Saturated Fat 1.7 g*
- *Cholesterol 78 mg*
- *Sodium 79 mg*
- *Total Carbs 1.8 g*
- *Fiber 1.1 g*
- *Sugar 0.3 g*
- *Protein 35 g*

Lentil Spinach Soup

Ingredients:

- 1/2 onion
- 2 carrots
- 1 rib celery
- 1 clove garlic
- 1 cup tomatoes, diced
- 1 teaspoon dried vegetable broth powder
- 1 teaspoon Sazon seasoning
- 1 cup red lentils
- 1 tablespoon lemon juice
- 3 cups alkaline water
- 1 bunch spinach

How to prepare:

1. Add all the vegetables to a greased pan.

2. Sauté for 5 minutes then add broth, tomatoes, and Sazon seasoning.
3. Mix well and stir in red lentils along with water.
4. Cook until lentil is soft and tender.
5. Add spinach and cook for 2 minutes.
6. Serve warm with lemon slices on top.

Preparation time: 05 minutes
Cooking time: 15 minutes
Total time: 20 minutes
Servings: 4

Nutritional Values:

- Calories 301
- Total Fat 12.2 g
- Saturated Fat 2.4 g
- Cholesterol 110 mg
- Sodium 276 mg
- Total Carbs 15 g
- Fiber 0.9 g
- Sugar 1.4 g
- Protein 28.8 g

Tangy Lentil Soup

Ingredients:

- 2 cups red lentils, picked over and rinsed
- 1 serrano Chile pepper, choppedchopped
- 1 large tomato, roughly choppedchopped
- 1 1 1/2-inch piece ginger, peeled and grated
- 3 cloves garlic, finely choppedchopped
- 1/4 teaspoon ground turmeric
- Sea salt, to taste

Topping

- 1/4 cup coconut yogurt

How to prepare:

1. Add lentils to a pot and with enough water to cover it.

2. Bring the lentils to a boil then reduce the heat.

3. Cook for 10 minutes on low simmer.

4. Stir in all the remaining ingredients.

5. Cook until lentils are soft and well mixed.

6. Garnish a dollop of coconut yogurt.

7. Serve.

Preparation time: 5 minutes

Cooking time: 15 minutes

Total time: 20 minutes

Servings: 4

Nutritional Values:

- *Calories 248*
- *Total Fat 2.4 g*
- *Saturated Fat 0.1 g*
- *Cholesterol 320 mg*
- *Sodium 350 mg*
- *Total Carbs 12.2 g*
- *Fiber 0.7 g*
- *Sugar 0.7 g*
- *Protein 44.3 g*

Vegetable Casserole

Ingredients:

- 2 large eggplants, peeled and sliced
- Sea salt, to taste
- 2 large cucumbers, diced
- 2 small green peppers, diced
- 1 Small red pepper, diced
- 1 Small yellow pepper, diced
- ¼ lb. green beans, sliced
- ½ cup olive oil
- 2 large sweet onions, Chopped
- 3 cloves garlic, crushed
- 2 yellow Squash, cubed

- 20 cherry tomatoes, halved
- ½ teaspoon sea salt
- ¼ teaspoon fresh ground pepper
- ¼ lb. lima beans (Optional)
- A handful of fresh chopped basil (Optional)
- ¼ cup alkaline water
- 1 cup fresh seasoned breadcrumbs

How to prepare:

1. Set your oven to 350 degrees F. Mix eggplant with salt and keep it aside.
2. Heat a greased skillet and sauté eggplant until evenly browned.
3. Transfer the eggplant to a plate.
4. Sauté onions in the same pan until soft.
5. Stir in garlic and cook for a minute then turn off the heat.
6. Layer a greased casserole dish with eggplants, green beans, cucumbers, peppers and yellow squash.
7. Add tomatoes, onion mixture, salt, and pepper.
8. Sprinkle seasoned breadcrumbs on top.
9. Bake for 1 hour and 30 minutes.
10. Serve.

Preparation time: 5 minutes
Cooking time: 1hr. 30 minutes

Total time: 1 hr. 35 minutes

Servings: 06

Nutritional Values:

- *Calories 372*
- *Total Fat 11.1 g*
- *Saturated Fat 5.8 g*
- *Cholesterol 610 mg*
- *Sodium 749 mg*
- *Total Carbs 0.9 g*
- *Fiber 0.2 g*
- *Sugar 0.2 g*
- *Protein 63.5 g*

Mushroom Leek Soup

Ingredients:

- 3 tablespoons vegetable oil, divided
- 2 ¾ cups leeks, finely chopped
- 3 garlic cloves, finely minced
- 7 cups assorted mushrooms, cleaned and sliced
- 5 tablespoons almond flour
- ¾ teaspoon sea salt
- ½ teaspoon ground black pepper
- 1 tablespoon fresh dill, very finely minced (optional)
- 3 cups vegetable broth
- 2/3 cup coconut cream
- ½ cup almond milk
- 1 ½ tablespoons sherry vinegar

How to prepare:

1. Heat oil in a Dutch oven and sauté garlic and leeks until soft.
2. Stir in mushrooms and sauté for 10 minutes.
3. Add flour, pepper, dill, and salt.
4. Mix well and cook for 2 minutes.
5. Pour in broth and cook to boil.
6. Reduce the heat and add the remaining ingredients.
7. Serve warm with almond flour bread.

Preparation time: 5 minutes

Cooking time: 8 minutes

Total time: 13 minutes

Servings: 4

Nutritional Values:

- *Calories 127*
- *Total Fat 3.5 g*
- *Saturated Fat 0.5 g*
- *Cholesterol 162 mg*
- *Sodium 142 mg*
- *Total Carbs 3.6g*
- *Fiber 0.4 g*
- *Sugar 0.5 g*
- *Protein 21.5 g*

Red Lentil Squash Soup

Ingredients:

- 1 yellow onion, chopped
- 2 tablespoons olive oil
- 1 large butternut squash, diced
- 1 1/2 cups red lentils
- 2 teaspoons dried sage
- 7 cups vegetable broth
- mineral sea salt & white or fresh cracked pepper, to taste

How to prepare:

1. Heat oil in a large stockpot.
2. Add onions and cook for 5 minutes.
3. Stir in squash and sage. Cook for 3 to 5 minutes.
4. Add broth, salt, pepper, and lentils.
5. Cook for 30 minutes on low heat.

6. Puree the mixture using a handheld blender.

7. Garnish with parsley and serve.

Preparation time: 5 minutes

Cooking time: 4 minutes

Total time: 9 minutes

Servings: 04

Nutritional Values:

- *Calories 323*
- *Total Fat 7.5 g*
- *Saturated Fat 1.1 g*
- *Cholesterol 20 mg*
- *Sodium 97 mg*
- *Total Carbs 21.4 g*
- *Fiber 0 g*
- *Sugar 0 g*
- *Protein 10.1g*

Cauliflower Potato Curry

Ingredients:

- 2 tablespoons vegetable oil
- 1 large onion, chopped
- a large piece of ginger , grated
- 3 garlic cloves, finely chopped
- ½ teaspoon turmeric
- 1 teaspoon ground cumin
- 1 teaspoon curry powder, or to taste
- 1 cup tomatoes, chopped
- ½ teaspoon sugar
- 1 cauliflower, cut into florets
- 2 potatoes, cut into chunks
- 1 small green chili, halved lengthways

- A squeeze of lemon juice
- Handful coriander, roughly chopped, to serve

How to prepare:

1. Add onion to a greased skillet and sauté until soft.
2. Stir in all the spices along with potatoes and cauliflower.
3. Sauté for 5 minutes then add tomatoes, sugar and green chilies.
4. Cover and cook for 30 minutes.
5. Serve warm with lemon juice and coriander.

Preparation time: 10 minutes
Cooking time: 35 minutes
Total time: 45 minutes
Servings: 04

Nutritional Values:

- *Calories 332*
- *Total Fat 7.5 g*
- *Saturated Fat 1.1 g*
- *Cholesterol 20 mg*
- *Sodium 97 mg*
- *Total Carbs 19.4 g*
- *Fiber 0 g*
- *Sugar 0 g*
- *Protein 3.1g*

Vegetable Bean Curry

Ingredients:

- 1 onion, finely chopped
- 4 garlic cloves, chopped
- 3 teaspoons coriander powder
- 1-1/2 teaspoons cinnamon powder
- 1 teaspoon ginger powder
- 1 teaspoon turmeric powder
- 1/2 teaspoon cayenne pepper
- 2 tablespoons tomato paste
- 1 tablespoon avocado oil
- 2 cans (15 ounces each) lima beans, rinsed and drained
- 3 cups sweet potatoes, cubed peeled
- 3 cups fresh cauliflower florets
- 4 medium carrots, diced

- 2 medium tomatoes, seeded and chopped
- 2 cups vegetable broth
- 1 cup light coconut milk
- 1/2 teaspoon pepper
- 1/4 teaspoon sea salt

How to prepare:
1. Heat oil in a slow cooker and add all the vegetables.
2. Stir in all the remaining ingredients.
3. Cook for 5 to 6 hours on low-temperature settings.
4. Serve warm.

Preparation time: 5 minutes
Cooking time: 6 hours
Total time: 6 hrs. 5 minutes
Servings: 08

Nutritional Values:
- *Calories 403*
- *Total Fat 12.5 g*
- *Saturated Fat 1.1 g*
- *Cholesterol 20 mg*
- *Sodium 397 mg*
- *Total Carbs 21.4 g*
- *Fiber 0 g*
- *Sugar 0 g*
- *Protein 8.1g*

Wild mushroom soup

Ingredients:

- 4 oz. almond butter
- 1 shallot, chopped
- 5 oz. portabella mushrooms, chopped
- 5 oz. oyster mushrooms, chopped
- 5 oz. shiitake mushrooms, chopped
- 1 garlic clove, minced
- ½ teaspoon dried thyme
- 3 cups alkaline water
- 1 vegetable bouillon cube
- 1 cup coconut cream
- ½ lb. celery root, chopped
- 1 tablespoon white wine vinegar
- Fresh parsley (optional)

How to prepare:

1. Melt butter in a cooking pan over medium heat.
2. Add vegetables to the pan and sauté until golden brown.
3. Stir in all the remaining ingredients to the pan and boil the mixture.
4. Reduce the heat to low and let it simmer for 15 minutes.
5. Add cream to the soup and puree it using a hand-held blender.
6. Serve warm with chopped parsley on top.

Preparation time: 10 minutes

Cooking time: 15 minutes

Total time: 25 minutes

Servings: 04

Nutritional Values:

- *Calories 243*
- *Total Fat 7.5 g*
- *Saturated Fat 1.1 g*
- *Cholesterol 20 mg*
- *Sodium 357 mg*
- *Total Carbs 14.4 g*
- *Fiber 0 g*
- *Sugar 0 g*
- *Protein 10.1g*

SNACK RECIPES

Pumpkin spice crackers

Ingredients:

- 1/3 cup coconut flour
- 2 tablespoons pumpkin pie spice
- 3/4 cup sunflower seeds
- 3/4 cup flaxseed
- 1/3 cup sesame seeds
- 1 tablespoon ground psyllium husk powder
- 1 teaspoon sea salt
- 3 tablespoons coconut oil, melted
- 11/3 cups alkaline water

How to prepare:

1. Set your oven to 300 degrees F.
2. Combine all dry ingredients in a bowl.

3. Add water and oil to the mixture and mix well.
4. Let the dough stay for 2 to 3 mins.
5. Spread the dough on a cookie sheet lined with parchment paper.
6. Bake for 30 minutes.
7. Reduce the oven heat to low and bake for another 30 minutes.
8. Crack the bread into bite-size pieces.
9. Serve

Preparation time: 10 minutes
Cooking time: 60 minutes
Total time: 70 minutes
Servings: 06

Nutritional Values:

- *Calories 248*
- *Total Fat 15.7 g*
- *Saturated Fat 2.7 g*
- *Cholesterol 75 mg*
- *Sodium 94 mg*
- *Total Carbs 0.4 g*
- *Fibre 0g*
- *Sugar 0 g*
- *Protein 24.9 g*

Spicy roasted nuts

Ingredients:

- 8 oz. pecans or almonds or walnuts
- 1 teaspoon sea salt
- 1 tablespoon olive oil or coconut oil
- 1 teaspoon ground cumin
- 1 teaspoon paprika powder or chili powder

How to prepare:

1. Add all the ingredients to a skillet.
2. Roast the nuts until golden brown.
3. Serve and enjoy.

Preparation time: 10 minutes
Cooking time: 15 minutes
Total time: 25 minutes
Servings: 4

Nutritional Values:

- *Calories 287*
- *Total Fat 29.5 g*
- *Saturated Fat 3 g*
- *Cholesterol 0 mg*
- *Total Carbs 5.9 g*
- *Sugar 1.4g*
- *Fiber 4.3 g*
- *Sodium 388 mg*
- *Protein 4.2 g*

Wheat Crackers

Ingredients:

1 3/4 cups almond flour

1 1/2 cups coconut flour

3/4 teaspoon sea salt

1/3 cup vegetable oil

1 cup alkaline water

Sea salt for sprinkling

How to prepare:

1. Set your oven to 350 degrees F.
2. Mix coconut flour, almond flour and salt in a bowl.
3. Stir in vegetable oil and water. Mix well until smooth.
4. Spread this dough on a floured surface into a thin sheet.
5. Cut small squares out of this sheet.

6. Arrange the dough squares on a baking sheet lined with parchment paper.
7. Bake for 20 minutes until light golden in color.
8. Serve.

Preparation time: 10 minutes

Cooking time: 20 minutes

Total time: 30 minutes

Servings: 4

Nutritional Values:

- *Calories 64*
- *Total Fat 9.2 g*
- *Saturated Fat 2.4 g*
- *Cholesterol 110 mg*
- *Sodium 276 mg*
- *Total Carbs 9.2 g*
- *Fiber 0.9 g*
- *Sugar 1.4 g*
- *Protein 1.5 g*

Potato Chips

Ingredients:

- 1 tablespoon vegetable oil
- 1 potato, sliced paper thin
- Sea salt, to taste

How to prepare:

1. Toss potato with oil and sea salt.
2. Spread the slices in a baking dish in a single layer.
3. Cook in a microwave for 5 minutes until golden brown.
4. Serve.

Preparation time: 10 minutes
Cooking time: 5 minutes
Total time: 15 minutes
Servings: 4

Nutritional Values:

- *Calories 80*
- *Total Fat 3.5 g*
- *Saturated Fat 0.1 g*
- *Cholesterol 320 mg*
- *Sodium 350 mg*
- *Total Carbs 11.6 g*
- *Fiber 0.7 g*
- *Sugar 0.7 g*
- *Protein 1.2 g*

Zucchini Pepper Chips

Ingredients:

- 1 2/3 cups vegetable oil
- 1 teaspoon garlic powder
- 1 teaspoon onion powder
- 1/2 teaspoon black pepper
- 3 tablespoons crushed red pepper flakes
- 2 zucchinis, thinly sliced

How to prepare:

1. Mix oil with all the spices in a bowl.
2. Add zucchini slices and mix well.
3. Transfer the mixture to a Ziplock bag and seal it.
4. Refrigerate for 10 minutes.
5. Spread the zucchini slices on a greased baking sheet.
6. Bake for 15 minutes
7. Serve.

Preparation time: 10 minutes

Cooking time: 15 minutes

Total time: 25 minutes

Servings: 04

Nutritional Values:

- *Calories 172*
- *Total Fat 11.1 g*
- *Saturated Fat 5.8 g*
- *Cholesterol 610 mg*
- *Sodium 749 mg*
- *Total Carbs 19.9 g*
- *Fiber 0.2 g*
- *Sugar 0.2 g*
- *Protein 13.5 g*

Apple Chips

Ingredients:

- 2 Golden Delicious apples, cored and thinly sliced
- 1 1/2 teaspoons white sugar
- 1/2 teaspoon ground cinnamon

How to prepare:

1. Set your oven to 225 degrees F.
2. Place apple slices on a baking sheet.
3. Sprinkle sugar an
4. d cinnamon over apple slices.
5. Bake for 45 minutes.
6. Serve

Preparation time: 5 minutes

Cooking time: 45 minutes

Total time: 50 minutes

Servings:4

Nutritional Values:

- *Calories 127*
- *Total Fat 3.5 g*
- *Saturated Fat 0.5 g*
- *Cholesterol 162 mg*
- *Sodium 142 mg*
- *Total Carbs 33.6g*
- *Fiber 0.4 g*
- *Sugar 0.5 g*
- *Protein 4.5 g*

Kale Crisps

Ingredients:

- 1 bunch kale, stems removed, leaves torn into even pieces
- 1 tablespoon olive oil
- 1 teaspoon sea salt

How to prepare:

1. Set your oven to 350 degrees F. Layer a baking sheet with parchment paper.
2. Spread the kale leaves on a paper towel to absorb all the moisture.
3. Toss the leaves with sea salt, and olive oil.
4. Spread them on the baking sheet and bake for 10 minutes.
5. Serve.

Preparation time: 10 minutes

Cooking time: 10 minutes

Total time: 20 minutes

Servings: 04

Nutritional Values:

- *Calories 113*
- *Total Fat 7.5 g*
- *Saturated Fat 1.1 g*
- *Cholesterol 20 mg*
- *Sodium 97 mg*
- *Total Carbs 1.4 g*
- *Fiber 0 g*
- *Sugar 0 g*
- *Protein 1.1g*

Carrot Chips

Ingredients:

- 4 carrots, washed, peeled and sliced
- 2 teaspoons extra-virgin olive oil
- 1/4 teaspoon sea salt

How to prepare:

1. Set your oven to 350 degrees F.
2. Toss carrots with salt and olive oil.
3. Spread the slices on two baking sheets in a single layer.
4. Bake for 6 minutes on upper and lower rack of the oven.
5. Switch the baking racks and bake for another 6 minutes.
6. Serve.

Preparation time: 5 minutes
Cooking time: 12 minutes

Total time: 17 minutes

Servings: 04

Nutritional Values:

- *Calories 153*
- *Total Fat 7.5 g*
- *Saturated Fat 1.1 g*
- *Cholesterol 20 mg*
- *Sodium 97 mg*
- *Total Carbs 20.4 g*
- *Fiber 0 g*
- *Sugar 0 g*
- *Protein 3.1g*

Pita Chips

Ingredients:

- 12 pita bread pockets, sliced into triangles
- 1/2 cup olive oil
- 1/2 teaspoon ground black pepper
- 1 teaspoon garlic salt
- 1/2 teaspoon dried basil
- 1 teaspoon dried chervil

How to prepare:

1. Set your oven to 400 degrees F.
2. Toss pita with all the remaining ingredients in a bowl.
3. Spread the seasoned triangles on a baking sheet.
4. Bake for 7 minutes until golden brown.
5. Serve with your favorite hummus.

Preparation time: 5 minutes

Cooking time: 7 minutes

Total time: 12 minutes

Servings: 04

Nutritional Values:

- *Calories 201*
- *Total Fat 5.5 g*
- *Saturated Fat 2.1 g*
- *Cholesterol 10 mg*
- *Sodium 597 mg*
- *Total Carbs 2.4 g*
- *Fiber 0 g*
- *Sugar 0 g*
- *Protein 3.1g*

Sweet Potato Chips

Ingredients:

- 1 sweet potato, thinly sliced
- 2 teaspoons olive oil, or as needed
- Coarse sea salt, to taste

How to prepare:

1. Toss sweet potato with oil and salt.
2. Spread the slices in a baking dish in a single layer.
3. Cook in a microwave for 5 minutes until golden brown.
4. Serve.

Preparation time: 5 minutes
Cooking time: 5 minutes
Total time: 10 minutes
Servings: 04

Nutritional Values:

- *Calories 213*
- *Total Fat 8.5 g*
- *Saturated Fat 3.1 g*
- *Cholesterol 120 mg*
- *Sodium 497 mg*
- *Total Carbs 21.4 g*
- *Fiber 0 g*
- *Sugar 0 g*
- *Protein 0.1g*

DESSERT RECIPES

Chocolate Crunch Bars

Ingredients:

- 1 1/2 cups sugar-free chocolate chips
- 1 cup almond butter
- Stevia to taste
- 1/4 cup coconut oil
- 3 cups pecans , chopped

How to prepare:

1. Layer an 8-inch baking pan with parchment paper.
2. Mix chocolate chips with butter, coconut oil, and sweetener in a bowl.
3. Melt it by heating in a microwave for 2 to 3 minutes until well mixed.
4. Stir in nuts and seeds. Mix gently.

5. Pour this batter into the baking pan and spread evenly.

6. Refrigerate for 2 to 3 hours.

7. Slice and serve.

Preparation time: 5 minutes

Cooking time: 5 minutes

Total time: 10 minutes

Servings: 04

Nutritional Values:

- *Calories 316*
- *Total Fat 30.9 g*
- *Saturated Fat 8.1 g*
- *Cholesterol 0 mg*
- *Total Carbs 8.3 g*
- *Sugar 1.8 g*
- *Fiber 3.8 g*
- *Sodium 8 mg*
- *Protein 6.4 g*

Peanut Butter Bars

Ingredients:

- 3/4 cup almond flour
- 2 oz. almond butter
- 1/4 cup Swerve
- 1/2 cup peanut butter
- 1/2 teaspoon vanilla

How to prepare:

1. Combine all the ingredients for bars.
2. Transfer this mixture to 6-inch small pan. Press it firmly.
3. Refrigerate for 30 minutes.
4. Slice and serve.

Preparation time: 10 minutes
Cooking time: 10 minutes

Total time: 20 minutes

Servings: 6

Nutritional Values:

- *Calories 214*
- *Total Fat 19 g*
- *Saturated Fat 5.8 g*
- *Cholesterol 15 mg*
- *Total Carbs 6.5 g*
- *Sugar 1.9 g*
- *Fiber 2.1 g*
- *Sodium 123 mg*
- *Protein 6.5 g*

Homemade Protein Bar

Ingredients:

- 1 cup nut butter
- 4 tablespoons coconut oil
- 2 scoops vanilla protein
- Stevia, to taste
- ½ teaspoon sea salt

Optional Ingredients:

- 1 teaspoon cinnamon

How to prepare:

1. Mix coconut oil with butter, protein, stevia, and salt in a dish.

2. Stir in cinnamon and chocolate chip.

3. Press the mixture firmly and freeze until firm.

4. Cut the crust into small bars.

5. Serve and enjoy.

Preparation time: 05 minutes

Cooking time: 10 minutes

Total time: 15 minutes

Servings: 4

Nutritional Values:

- *Calories 179*
- *Total Fat 15.7 g*
- *Saturated Fat 8 g*
- *Cholesterol 0 mg*
- *Total Carbs 4.8 g*
- *Sugar 3.6 g*
- *Fiber 0.8 g*
- *Sodium 43 mg*
- *Protein* 5.6 g

Shortbread Cookies

Ingredients:

- 2 1/2 cups almond flour
- 6 tablespoons nut butter
- 1/2 cup erythritol
- 1 teaspoon vanilla essence

How to prepare:

1. Preheat your oven to 350 degrees F.
2. Layer a cookie sheet with parchment paper.
3. Beat butter with erythritol until fluffy.
4. Stir in vanilla essence and almond flour. Mix well until crumbly.
5. Spoon out a tablespoon of cookie dough onto the cookie sheet.
6. Add more dough to make as many cookies.
7. Bake for 15 minutes until brown.
8. Serve.

Preparation time: 10 minutes

Cooking time: 70 minutes

Total time: 80 minutes

Servings: 6

Nutritional Values:

- *Calories 288*
- *Total Fat 25.3 g*
- *Saturated Fat 6.7 g*
- *Cholesterol 23 mg*
- *Total Carbs 9.6 g*
- *Sugar 0.1 g*
- *Fiber 3.8 g*
- *Sodium 74 mg*
- *Potassium 3 mg*
- *Protein 7.6 g*

Coconut Chip Cookies

Ingredients:

- 1 cup almond flour
- ½ cup cacao nibs
- ½ cup coconut flakes, unsweetened
- 1/3 cup erythritol
- ½ cup almond butter
- ¼ cup nut butter, melted
- ¼ cup almond milk
- Stevia, to taste
- ¼ teaspoon sea salt

How to prepare:

1. Preheat your oven to 350 degrees F.
2. Layer a cookie sheet with parchment paper.

3. Add and combine all the dry ingredients in a glass bowl.
4. Whisk in butter, almond milk, vanilla essence, stevia, and almond butter.
5. Beat well then stir in dry mixture. Mix well.
6. Spoon out a tablespoon of cookie dough on the cookie sheet.
7. Add more dough to make as many as 16 cookies.
8. Flatten each cookie using your fingers.
9. Bake for 25 minutes until golden brown.
10. Let them sit for 15 minutes.
11. Serve.

Preparation time: 10 minutes
Cooking time: 15 minutes
Total time: 25 minutes
Servings: 04

Nutritional Values:
- Calories 192
- Total Fat 17.44 g
- Saturated Fat 11.5 g
- Cholesterol 125 mg
- Total Carbs 2.2 g
- Sugar 1.4 g
- Fiber 2.1 g
- Sodium 135 mg
- Protein 4.7 g

Coconut Cookies

Ingredients:

- 6 tablespoons coconut flour
- ¾ teaspoons baking powder
- 1/8 teaspoon sea salt
- 3 tablespoons nut butter
- 1/6 cup coconut oil
- 6 tablespoon swerve
- 1/3 cup coconut milk
- 1/2 teaspoon vanilla essence

How to prepare:

1. Preheat your oven to 375 degrees F.
2. Layer a cookie sheet with parchment paper.
3. Beat all the wet ingredients in a mixer.

4. Mix all the dry mixture in a blender.

5. Stir in the wet mixture and mix well until smooth.

6. Spoon a tablespoon of cookie dough on the cookie sheet.

7. Add more dough to make as many cookies.

8. Bake for 8 to 10 minutes until golden brown.

9. Serve.

Preparation time: 10 minutes

Cooking time: 20 minutes

Total time: 30 minutes

Servings: 6

Nutritional Values:

- *Calories 151*
- *Total Fat 13.4 g*
- *Saturated Fat 7 g*
- *Cholesterol 20 mg*
- *Total Carbs 6.4 g*
- *Sugar 2.1 g*
- *Fiber 4.8 g*
- *Sodium 136 mg*
- *Protein 4.2 g*

Berry Mousse

Ingredients:

- 1 teaspoon lemon zest
- 3 oz. raspberries or blueberries
- ¼ teaspoon vanilla essence
- 2 cups coconut cream

How to prepare:

1. Blend cream in an electric mixer until fluffy.
2. Stir in vanilla and lemon zest. Mix well.
3. Fold in nuts and berries.
4. Cover the bowl with a plastic wrap.
5. Refrigerate for 3 hours.
6. Garnish as desired.
7. Serve.

Preparation time: 10 minutes

Cooking time: 25 minutes

Total time: 35 minutes

Servings: 04

Nutritional Values:

- *Calories 265*
- *Total Fat 13 g*
- *Saturated Fat 10.2 g*
- *Cholesterol 09 mg*
- *Total Carbs 7.5 g*
- *Sugar 1.1 g*
- *Fiber 0.5 g*
- *Sodium 7.1 mg*
- *Protein 5.2 g*

Almond Pulp Cookies

Ingredients:

- 3 cups almond pulp
- 1 Granny Smith apple
- 1-2 teaspoon cinnamon
- 2-3 tablespoons raw honey
- 1/4 cup coconut flakes

How to prepare:

1. Blend almond pulp with remaining ingredients in a food processor.
2. Make small cookies out this mixture.
3. Placethem on a cookie sheet, lined with parchment paper.
4. Place the sheet in a food dehydrator for 6 to 10 hours at 115 degrees F.
5. Serve.

Preparation time: 5 minutes

Cooking time: 10 hrs.

Total time: 10hrs 5 minutes

Servings: 04

Nutritional Values:

- *Calories 240*
- *Total Fat 22.5 g*
- *Saturated Fat 2.7 g*
- *Cholesterol 15 mg*
- *Sodium 474 mg*
- *Total Carbs 17.3 g*
- *Fibre 0g*
- *Sugar 0 g*
- *Protein 14.9 g*

Avocado Pudding

Ingredients:

- 2 avocados
- 3/4-1 cup almond milk
- 1/3-1/2 cup raw cacao powder
- 1 teaspoon 100% pure organic vanilla (optional)
- 2-4 tablespoons Swerve Sweetener

How to prepare:
1. Blend all the ingredients in a blender.
2. Refrigerate for 4 hours in a container.
3. Serve.

Preparation time: 10 minutes

Cooking time: 0 minutes

Total time: 10 minutes

Servings: 2

Nutritional Values:

- *Calories 609*
- *Total Fat 50.5 g*
- *Saturated Fat 11.7 g*
- *Cholesterol 58 mg*
- *Sodium 2463 mg*
- *Total Carbs 9.9 g*
- *Fiber 1.5 g*
- *Sugar 0.3 g*
- *Protein 29.3 g*

Coconut Raisins cookies

Ingredients:

- 1 1/4 cup almond flour
- 1 cup coconut flour
- 1 teaspoon baking soda
- 1/2 teaspoon Celtic sea salt
- 1 cup nut butter
- 1 cup coconut palm sugar
- 2 teaspoons vanilla
- ¼ cup almond milk
- 3/4 cup organic raisins
- 3/4 cup coconut chips or flakes

How to prepare:

1. Set your oven to 357 degrees F.
2. Mix flour with salt and baking soda.

3. Blend butter with sugar until creamy then stirs in almond milk and vanilla.
4. Mix well then stir in dry mixture. Mix until smooth.
5. Fold in all the remaining ingredients.
6. Make small cookies out this dough.
7. Arrange the cookies on a baking sheet.
8. Bake for 10 minutes until golden brown.

Preparation time: 10 minutes

Cooking time: 10 minutes

Total time: 20 minutes

Servings: 4

Nutritional Values:

- *Calories 237*
- *Total Fat 19.8 g*
- *Saturated Fat 1.4 g*
- *Cholesterol 10 mg*
- *Sodium 719 mg*
- *Total Carbs 55.1 g*
- *Fiber 0.9 g*
- *Sugar 1.4 g*
- *Protein 17.8 g*

10 Days Meal Plan:

Day 01
Breakfast: Crunchy Quinoa Meal
Snack: Pink Smoothie
Lunch: Cabbage with Coconut and Sweet Potato
Snack: Zucchini Chips
Dinner: Red Lentil Squash Soup
Dessert: Coconut Raisins Cookies

Day 02
Breakfast: Millet Porridge
Snack: Green Smoothie
Lunch: Cauliflower Curry Soup
Snack: Kale Crisps
Dinner: Cauliflower Potato Curry
Dessert: Avocado Pudding

Day 03
Breakfast: Zucchini Muffins
Snack: Detox Berries Smoothie
Lunch: Peach Panzanella
Snack: Carrot Chips
Dinner: Mushroom Leek soup
Dessert: Almond Pulp Cookies

Day 04
Breakfast: Amaranth Porridge
Snack: Cinnamon Berry Smoothie

Lunch: Carrot Sweet Potato Soup
Snack: Pumpkin Spice Crackers
Dinner: Vegetable Casserole
Dessert: Berry Mousse

Day 05
Breakfast: Quinoa Porridge
Snack: Cranberry Smoothie
Lunch: Rosemary Roasted Yams
Snack: Carrot Chips
Dinner: Wild Mushroom Soup
Dessert: Coconut Cookies

Day 06
Breakfast: Zucchini Pancakes
Snack: Apple Almond Smoothie
Lunch: Green Bean Stir-fry
Snack: Potato Chips
Dinner: Tangy Lentil Soup
Dessert: Coconut Chip Cookies

Day 07
Breakfast: Banana Barley Porridge
Snack: Green Tea Blueberry Smoothie
Lunch: Quinoa Vegetable Soup
Snack: Pita Crackers
Dinner: Mixed Vegetable Bean Curry
Dessert: Shortbread Cookies

Day 08
Breakfast: Pumpkin Spice Quinoa
Snack: Apple Ginger Smoothie
Lunch: Zucchini Lasagna
Snack: Spicy Roasted Nuts
Dinner: Lentil Spinach Soup
Dessert: Homemade Protein Bars

Day 09
Breakfast: Tofu Vegetable Fry
Snack: Green Apple Smoothie
Lunch: Veggies with Mushrooms
Snack: Wheat Crackers
Dinner: Carrot and Golden Beet Soup
Dessert: Peanut Butter Bars

Day 10
Breakfast: Almond Flour Pancakes
Snack: Avocado Smoothie
Lunch: Sprout Onion Fry
Snack: Apple Chips
Dinner: Sweet Potato Green Soup
Dessert: Chocolate Crunch Bars

Conclusion

The aim of this cookbook was to introduce the readers with most of the insight regarding alkaline diet in a comprehensive manner. The text of this book has been categorized into different sections, each discussing the basics, details, haves and have-nots and the alkaline diet-related recipes. The chapter for recipes is divided into subsections, ranging from breakfast to lunch, dinner, smoothies, snacks, and desserts. So spare some time to go through the length of this book and experience the miraculous effects of an alkaline diet on your mind and health.

31156827R00095

Made in the USA
San Bernardino, CA
02 April 2019